Corythosaurus

Styracosaurus

Coelophysis

Triceratops

Diplodocus

Saltopus

...plodocus stretched 84 feet, about the length of five big cars parked end to end. Saltopus measured only 28 inches long.

Dinosaurs

By Kathryn Jackson
Paintings by Jay H. Matternes

Books for Young Explorers

NATIONAL GEOGRAPHIC SOCIETY

COMMON JURASSIC & CRETACEOUS DINOSAURS

The skeleton of a dinosaur
is a strange and mysterious sight.
   But dinosaurs were strange animals.
   And mysterious ones, too.
   They were huge reptiles that lived long,
long before there were people on earth.
   In those days, reptiles swam in the seas.
   They flew in the air.
   And walked on the land.
   But the reptiles that ruled the land
were the dinosaurs.
   And there were dinosaurs of many kinds.
   Most of them ate plants.
   But some ate other dinosaurs.
   There were dinosaurs that lived
in green swamps and shady forests.
   And on wide plains and dry deserts.
   The dinosaurs were lords of the earth
for millions and millions of years.
   But that did not happen overnight.
   It took a long, slow time.

Other reptiles were living on earth long, long before the days of the dinosaurs.

But—like all living things—they needed water to stay alive.

So they had to stay in the wet, green swamps.

Then along came the swift little thecodonts.

They ran on their long hind legs—like birds.
And they did not have to stay in the water
because they stored it in their scaly bodies.
So they could live and hunt where they wished.
The thecodonts—reptiles only four feet long—
were the ancestors of all the dinosaurs.

Millions of years
rolled slowly by.
And at last the days
of the dinosaurs are here.

There are strange plants
growing near the ponds.
Many insects scuttle about.
And small reptiles that look
much like the thecodonts
are running here and there.
One finds a tasty lizard.
It pounces on it and runs away.
But a big, wily reptile is watching.
With one strike of its long jaws,
it pulls the small reptile down
into the water—to eat.
The water bubbles.
And the small reptile is gone.
It was Saltopus—one of the
first of the dinosaurs.

6

SALT-o-pus

But so it goes.

Dinosaurs come and dinosaurs go in this wild, green world of eat-or-be-eaten.

And each kind has ways of its own.

ter-at-o-SAWR-us

PLAT-e-o-sawr

The big, peaceful plateosaurs eat plants.

They chew away with peglike teeth.

And they watch for enemies with their big birdlike eyes.

At every sound, they get ready to run.

For fierce Teratosaurus eats other dinosaurs, and he may be hunting plateosaurs right now.

Coelophysis is small and fierce.
Like other meat-eaters, he has his own hunting grounds.
But look—he sees another Coelophysis hunting there.
No meat-eater will stand for that!
So Coelophysis looks just as fierce as he can,
and the other small dinosaur turns tail—and runs away.

9

see-lo-FI-sis

The days and years roll by.
The early dinosaurs are gone now.
Bigger ones have taken their place.

al-lo-SAWR-us

The mighty Allosaurus is hungry.
So here he is—tracking some huge plant-eaters.
They are brontosaurs, coming home
from the secret place where they lay their eggs.
For safety, they often travel together.
But one is lagging behind the herd.
Allosaurus strides closer and closer.
Then—just at the last moment—the lone brontosaur
splashes deep into the river.
There she is safe, for meat-eaters are not built
to go in the water.

BRONT-o-sawr

12

brak-e-o-SAWR-us

Now an enormous dinosaur lumbers out of the water.

It is Brachiosaurus, the biggest plant-eater of all times.

He is as heavy as seven elephants, and his head towers a good forty feet in the air.

Diplodocus are feeding farther out.

Down go their heads, to tear off tender plants.

Then up they come—to gulp a dripping mouthful.

All the long day, their heads go up and down, up and down.

dip-LAH-do-kus

The days and years keep rolling by.

Earth has changed again.
There are flowering plants.
And small, furry animals.
And there are more dinosaurs
than ever before.
Here is small Thescelosaurus
that runs as fast as a deer.
And Styracosaurus—
with his strong, spiked shield.
Other plant-eaters have armor.
Or sharp, curved beaks.
Still others have terrible horns.
Now the plant-eaters have many
new ways to protect themselves.

thes-el-o-SAWR-us

For this is the time of huge meat-eaters—
the biggest ever to walk the earth.

sty-rak-o-SAWR-us

tih-ran-o-SAWR-us rex

The biggest of all the meat-eaters
is Tyrannosaurus Rex — the king
of the tyrant reptiles.

His head alone is four feet long,
and his teeth are as sharp as daggers.

He runs on long, powerful hind legs —
but look at his tiny front legs!

Hungry as he is, Tyrannosaurus Rex
cannot turn Ankylosaurus over.
Nor can he bite through that tough armor.
Ankylosaurus swings his heavy knobbed tail —
and Tyrannosaurus Rex hurries out of its way.
He goes to the swamps to hunt.

an-ky-lo-SAWR-us

Here the duckbill dinosaurs are feeding.
They scoop up water plants with their wide, flat bills.
The strange crests on the duckbills' heads are hollow.
They are a part of their noses — so perhaps the duckbills
can smell an enemy from far away.

Prosaurolophus
(pro-sawr-AH-lof-us)

kor-ith-o-SAWR-us

Corythosaurus sniffs, and smells Tyrannosaurus Rex.
At once, the duckbills scramble into the water.
Webbed feet paddling — and strong tails swishing —
they all swim swiftly away.
When Tyrannosaurus Rex comes, they are out of reach.
So on he goes — to hunt in the dry uplands.

Lambeosaurus
(lam-be-o-SAWR-us)

Parasaurolophus
(par-a-sawr-AH-lof-us)

Here live the one-horned Monoclonius.

They see Tyrannosaurus Rex coming, and make
a big circle around their young.

It is a fort of bony shields and sharp beaks.

Few enemies would try to break through it.

mon-o-KLON-e-us

Not even the mighty Tyrannosaurus Rex.
By now, he is wild with hunger.
And his strong eyes spot the meat he wants.
It is Triceratops, the great three-horned plant-eater,
the biggest of all the horned dinosaurs.

For a moment—a moment of terrible silence—
the two great dinosaurs size each other up.
Then Tyrannosaurus Rex charges.
And Triceratops wheels to face his charge.
The great monsters clash—and clash again.

Their thick, scaly hides are not easy to tear,
but the meat-eater's teeth are long and sharp.
Triceratops is hurt—and bleeding.
Panting, he sinks to the trampled ground.
Now Tyrannosaurus Rex will have meat to eat!

try-SER-a-tops

But wait—the tyrant king is wounded, too.
Gored by sharp horns, he staggers and falls
beside his enemy.
The savage fight is over.
And the hot, slow-moving sun has set
on the long days of the dinosaurs.

In time, nothing was left of the dinosaurs
but bones, teeth, and eggshells.
And footprints the dinosaurs had made.
Some became fossils.
They were buried in age-old rock, and there
they stayed for many millions of years.

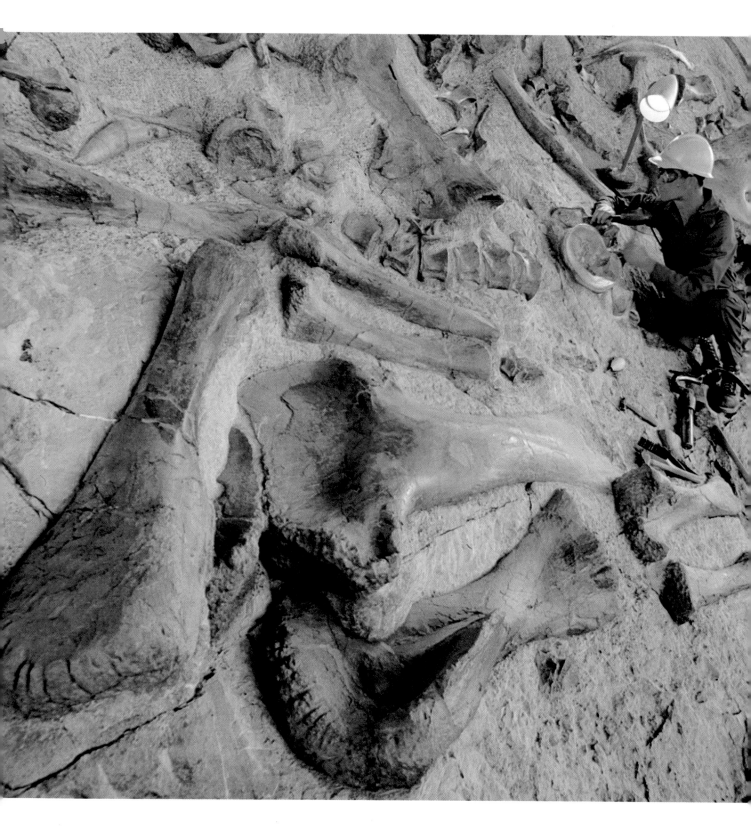

Less than two hundred years ago, people found some
of the dinosaur fossils.

Scientists had studied fossils,
but never any so huge!

Eagerly, people began to hunt for more dinosaur fossils.

In time, they found many.

They found
the enormous bones
of Brontosaurus.

And deep footprints
made by dinosaurs.

They found eggs
of Protoceratops.

They even
found the prints
of strange plants
that grew in the days
of the dinosaurs.

Scientists may work for months, even years,
when they find dinosaur fossils.

Huge rocks, with the fossils still in them,
are cut out of the earth around them.

Fossils are brittle—they break easily.

So workmen gently wrap them,
and let the covering harden
before moving them to a laboratory.

Next, the fossils are scraped and cleaned.
And studied by scientists.
The pieces of a skeleton are carefully matched.
When a piece is missing, scientists copy that part
from another skeleton.

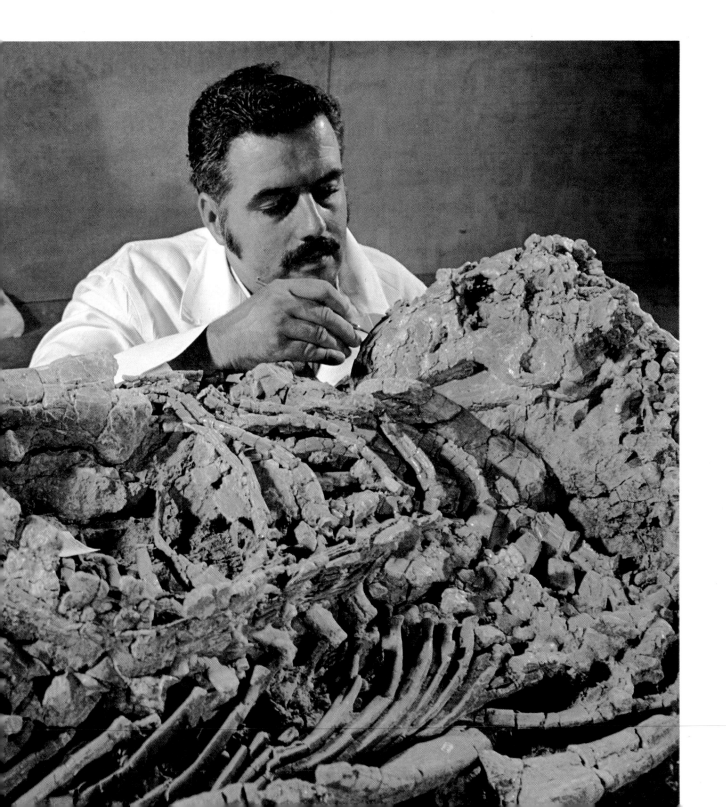

At last, the whole skeleton
of a dinosaur slowly takes shape.
    And as the scientists work, the story
of the dinosaurs slowly unfolds.
    Much is known.
    But much is still unknown.
    No one knows how the last dinosaurs
died—or why they died.
    Did earth grow too cold or hot?
    Did other animals crowd them out?
    Or did an exploding star in space
end the days of the dinosaurs?
    No one knows.
    Even today, scientists are still finding
and studying dinosaur fossils.
    One day, the whole story may unfold.

    Or perhaps it will always be hidden.
    And as strange and mysterious as any
dinosaur skeleton you can see today.

Prepared by the Special Publications Division of the National Geographic Society
Melvin M. Payne, President; Melville Bell Grosvenor, Editor-in-Chief; Gilbert M. Grosvenor, Editor.

Photographic Credits

Donald J. Crump, National Geographic Staff (page 1); Mickey Pfleger (2-3, 27 top, bottom); National Geographic Photographer James L. Stanfield (26-27); Nathan Benn (27 middle); Michael D. Hoover (28); Ivan Massar, Black Star (28-29); Joseph H. Bailey, National Geographic Staff (30-31).

Endsheets: Jay H. Matternes

Plateosaurus

Stegosaur*

Tyrannosaurus Rex

Ankylosaurus

Thescelosaurus

Dinosaurs came in many sizes: Styracosaurus (upper right) stood just over six feet—a few inches taller than an average man to